If You Want Different Do Different

Todd Baker

Divine Destiny Publishing

Copyright © 2025 by Todd Baker and Divine Destiny Publishing

All Rights Reserved. Apart from any fair dealing for the purposes of research or private study, or criticism or review, as permitted under the Copyright, Designs and Patents Act 1988, this publication may only be reproduced, stored or transmitted, in any form or by any means, with the prior permission in writing of the copyright owner, or in the case of the reprographic reproduction in accordance with the terms of licensees issued by the Copyright Licensing Agency. Enquiries concerning reproduction outside those terms should be sent to the publisher.

Dedication

This book is written for my son and daughter, Noah and Macy. You are two of the most amazing human beings I know. Responsible, respectful, and fully engaged in creating your own lives every single day.

You're still discovering who you are and who you want to be, and you're doing it with intention. Watching your journey unfold has been one of the greatest privileges of my life. I'm so proud of who you are and how you carry yourselves with your friends, your family, and everyone around you.

Truthfully, I've learned more from you than you will ever know. Just by watching you grow, adapt, and lead with quiet strength. You've inspired me in ways I could never have predicted. This journey toward better health and staying active started because of you and continues today, still fueled by your presence in my life.

As my goals evolve and I strive for more, you are always the reason behind the fire. You're the first thought I have each morning when I reflect on what's going right in my life.

You are growing up in a world very different from the one I knew, with new pressures, distractions, and demands on your time. And yet, you've remained grounded, focused, and true to what matters most.

Noah and Macy, I love you both more than you can imagine. I can't wait to witness the future versions of yourselves you are building each and every day.

If you want different, do different.

Contents

Foreword By Kris Ashley	vii
Foreword By Laban Ditchburn	xi
Introduction	xv
1. My Background and Stories	1
2. Mindset	9
3. Purpose & Clarity	23
4. Inspiration	29
5. Importance of Ritual	33
6. No Such Thing as Failure	37
7. Grow, Every Single Day in Every Possible Way	43
8. Realization	49
9. Simple, Not Easy	55
10. If You Want Different, Do Different	61
11. Bridge	65
12. Don't Have Dreams, Have Goals	71
13. Go, NOW!	75
14. Challenges	79
15. Alone	91
16. Success Stories	95
17. Conclusion	99
Resources	108
About Todd Baker	109

Foreword By Kris Ashley

When Todd asked me to write the foreword for his book, I was deeply honored and also excited. As someone who has been immersed in the world of personal development for over two decades, I have read countless books on the subject matter. This one stands out for several reasons.

I first met Todd when I was a guest on his podcast while promoting my own book. We immediately clicked not only because we are on a similar career trajectory, but also because of our similar outlook on life. I immediately invited Todd to come on my own podcast to continue our conversation, as it was clear that he possessed not only a dedication to his own personal growth but also a passion for helping others. He truly walks the walk and lives by the principles he shares in this book. In the time that I have known him, I have watched him step outside of his comfort zone to propel his life forward. Not only is he an inspirational leader in that respect, but he also truly cares about others. Countless times he has offered to make connections for me or send new content my way because he knows that when one of us does better, we all do better.

If You Want Different, Do Different is a reflection of Todd's deep commitment to mindset work and his own lived experiences. It is the perfect pocket-sized, no-fluff handbook that will guide you to courageously step forward into the life you desire. What sets this book apart is its straightforward approach, broken into easily digestible sections and lists. Todd takes lofty ideas and breaks them down beautifully in a way that makes them simple to not only understand, but also to put into action. His examples are relatable, and he gently encourages the reader to change their outlook.

For anyone seeking to transform their life, better their relationships, advance their career, or improve their health, this book offers practical advice, personal anecdotes, and inspirational stories. The title itself sums it up well, and those six simple words have the capacity to completely change your life.

I encourage you to dive into this book with an open mind and a willingness to turn the lens inward and examine where you're at, what led you to this moment, and the steps needed to get you to where you want to go next. Personal development is a journey, and starting with the right tools, like those provided here, can lead you to great new heights.

I have no doubt that *If You Want Different, Do Different* will be a resource you visit again and again. And I am confident that Todd's wisdom will speak to you for years to come and serve as a reminder that all it takes is one small step to radically change the trajectory of your life.

With care and gratitude,

Kris Ashley

Author of *Change Your Mind To Change Your Reality: How Shifting Your Thinking Can Unlock Your Health, Your Relationships, and Your Peace of Mind*

Foreword By Laban Ditchburn

Have you ever felt so trapped in a dysfunctional cycle of life, knowing deep down that YOU are capable of so much more? This book is part of your key to help break free from that rut.

I first met Todd during a time when I was exploring new ways to inspire and uplift others. His story resonated deeply with me immediately. Todd's willful and blind dedication to personal growth and his commitment to helping others transform their lives make his work truly significant to me.

The central theme of *If You Want Different, Do Different* will become apparent as you delve into Todd's own personal and powerful anecdotes. But fundamentally, what came across to me was centered on embracing necessary change and taking bold, massive, and courageous action so that you can facilitate your own miraculous outcomes.

Becoming your own superhero is probably a more accurate description...

In a world (read this part aloud in your best Don LaFontaine movie voice) where many feel stuck or constrained by their circumstances, Todd's writings provide a super simple roadmap to freedom and fulfillment. It's a guide for anyone ready to break free from old patterns and pursue a more meaningful and purpose-driven life.

Todd's journey from addiction to enlightenment is a testament to his resilience and strength. His experiences, including overcoming personal challenges and transforming his life, add immense credibility to his teachings. Todd's work as a coach and mentor has impacted many lives, further establishing his expertise in personal development.

Reading *If You Want Different, Do Different* has been a transformative experience for me. Todd's insights on resilience, daily rituals, and viewing setbacks as learning opportunities are not just theoretical—they are lived and proven. His practical advice and inspirational stories resonate deeply, offering valuable lessons for anyone seeking change.

Finally, of all the many millions of books in the world, you just happen to be holding this one… so as you embark on this journey through *If You Want Different, Do Different,* remember this: "Coincidence is God's way of staying anonymous." So take that from Albert Einstein as the sign you need today to take action.

With courage,

Laban Ditchburn

World's Best Courage Coach and Author of *Bet on You,* an addiction recovery memoir-self-help book.

Introduction

Of all the pages, lessons, and stories contained in this book, I want everyone to take away one major message. If you want different, do different. I will go into more depth as we move forward but keep that thought and lesson at the forefront of what you take from this book. Let it be the starting point for creating the life you aspire to.

Also, I realize this is not the longest book and that it doesn't go on and on about every single topic discussed. That's intentional. Something I provide my clients is clarity and simplicity. With that, I share a lot of information to offer clarity, and I deliver it in a straightforward way to provide simplicity. There is already too much complexity in our lives. I didn't want to add to that with this book.

I am the proud parent of two active, responsible, driven kids. At the time of this writing, my son is eighteen and my daughter is sixteen. Both are active with friends, school, and sports, and they are figuring out who they are and what is important to them. They've always been involved in sports and outdoor activities, baseball and softball mainly. For all their similarities, they are different and unique individuals in their own right. My son is extremely athletic and takes on all sorts of challenges and new things when they're presented. My daughter is very creative and smarter than I could have imagined. She maintains a 4.0 in high school and, this year, her junior year, was invited into the National Honor Society.

I realize I may sound like the proud parent with a picture-perfect story, but that's not even remotely close to reality. When my son was born, he had breathing issues and spent the first week of his life in the NICU to get it under control. That was followed by numerous falls, cuts, and bruises due to skateboarding and bike riding, culminating in an accident where he fell, and the handlebars came off the scooter and hit his neck, just missing his esophagus. Later came the broken nose in high school from a bad hit straight to the face. Fortunately, the fracture was small and did not require surgery.

My daughter's story is similar, but her biggest challenge came when she was attacked by a neighbor's dog.

It went for her throat and nearly cost her everything. An amazing team of doctors, and our first helicopter ride, got us to the hospital, where the doctor explained how close the bite came to causing life-threatening injuries. In true resilient kid form, she toughed it out. She has no fear of dogs, and the scar can't really be seen unless you look for it. She is a thriving teenager.

Through all of this and my life so far, I've learned to slow down and be aware of everything happening around me. I've learned to take time to notice and appreciate not just the big, obvious things, but the little things. The breeze, the smells, the scenery, the people. Everything carries a lesson if we're willing to pause and take it in.

I've always been a naturally curious person, but that curiosity has grown as I've focused more on my own progress and growth. Opportunities are all around us, but we have to be aware and open to receive them. I hear people talk all the time about bad luck or that good things just don't happen to them. I completely disagree. What I've come to believe is that they are getting in their own way and preventing themselves from experiencing the great things that are right in front of them.

Something amazing happens when your mindset shifts from things happening to you to things happening for you. You become an attractor, and more and more possibilities start showing up. You recognize the opportunities that were always there.

A great example of this is how I got involved with the LA Tribune and their podcast network. It wasn't something I was seeking out or even knew was forming. I was approached with the opportunity because of my podcast. Next thing I knew, I was not only learning from some of the best in the business, but I also got to be a guest on the Think and Grow Rich Summit, based on the writings of Napoleon Hill. That guest list included people like Les Brown, Mark Victor Hansen, Bill Walsh, and many others. Again, this wasn't something I was chasing. It came to me, and I believe that happened because my mindset was open. I saw that things happen for me, not to me.

The thing I believe holds most people back from going after their goals and living the greatness they were designed for is not circumstance, upbringing, time, work, opportunity, or luck. It's themselves. These thoughts and limitations creep into their lives, settle in, and become their reality. They start to believe those limits cannot be overcome.

The most important thing we can do to take back control of our lives is to return to a positive, opportunity-seeking mindset. Setting goals and having aspirations is not as simple as writing them down on January first and getting to work. That often leads to falling short of what you truly want. Real progress takes consistent work, intentional thought, and purposeful action.

People tend to get short-sighted with goals. They focus on losing a certain number of pounds, making a specific percentage more money, or going out to dinner more often with their significant other. But the challenge is that you have to repeat that process year after year. And if you fall short even once, you start playing catch-up.

Instead of focusing on the next twelve months, focus on the rest of your life. Instead of focusing on losing fifteen pounds, focus on becoming fit. Fitness and activity should be part of your everyday life. By shifting to a long-term mindset, you take the pressure off the daily checklist and step into a sustainable rhythm. Some days, a simple walk is enough to clear the mind and remind you of what really matters.

This book is filled with ideas about mindset, clarity of purpose, inspiration, and other thoughts that can support you on your path. I believe every person is born with greatness, but many never tap into it. For so many reasons, they fall short and live a life full of "what ifs." Taking control of your future and making daily progress toward your vision of prosperity is something that belongs to you. Use what's here. Take what fits your life, your goals, and your way of living your best life.

And above all, if you are not living that life today, do something about it. Don't get stuck in circumstance or continue to make excuses about why it won't work. In coaching, I hear people explain what they believe are reasons for not making a change. But more often than not, they're just excuses in disguise.

So instead of thinking about why something won't work, imagine what your life will look like when it does. Who will you be? What will your life feel like when you are fully living it?

Whatever that life looks like, wherever you are now, and whatever it will take to get there, know this: If you want different, do different.

Don't be like the fly hitting the glass, thinking that if you try just one more time, the window will open. Don't wait for something or someone to change your life. Make it happen. You already know what's not working. Look at it. Be honest with yourself. Then figure out what's missing and act on it.

That doesn't mean you have to take wild chances or leap before you're ready. It just means doing different, whatever that looks like for you, your goals, your schedule, your responsibilities, your risk tolerance, and your skill set. Remember, real growth and meaningful goals are about the long game.

That brings me to another idea that will come up again throughout this book and in my coaching. Make progress and grow every single day in every possible way.

You should have huge goals. Don't think small. Make your goals about your lifetime. Instead of focusing on losing ten pounds this year, focus on becoming active and staying fit for life. That's something you can build toward daily, and it will last a lifetime.

Your comparison should not be what you see on TV, social media, or in your neighbor's backyard. Your only comparison should be to yourself from the day before.

The goal is to get one percent better every day. It may not sound like much, but here's some perspective: one percent better every day for a year makes you thirty-seven times better than when you started. That's massive. And it's doable. You can make small, focused improvements every day.

So I ask you to imagine, what kind of life would you be living if you improved by one percent every day for the next decade, or four?

Of all the thoughts, stories, and ideas in this book, let this one rise to the top.

If you want different, do different.

Chapter 1

My Background and Stories

Growing up in the suburbs west of Denver, my younger brother, younger sister, and I had a great upbringing. We were always active, my brother and I playing baseball and football, and my sister playing soccer. Our parents got us into a ski club during the winter, and we spent weekends camping, fishing, and exploring the mountains, often while traveling for sports. I realize that may sound a bit idyllic, and in many ways it was, but my childhood wasn't without challenges. We had our fair share of bumps, bruises, and moments of getting in trouble for doing the kinds of stupid things kids do.

One of the biggest challenges I had in elementary school was dislocating my throwing shoulder while playing. That pain and inconvenience stuck with me.

Another memory that stands out is riding bikes with a friend who decided to try riding with no hands. The front tire twisted, and he went over the handlebars, face-first onto the pavement. I still remember looking at him afterward and not recognizing him at first because of the injury to his face. Thankfully, he recovered fully but never tried riding with no hands again. My mom worked as a teacher's aide in the elementary school, so anytime I got into trouble, she found out. I always knew what kind of conversation I'd be having that night.

Junior high was fairly uneventful. I kept playing sports and started taking the school bus once a month to go skiing. One notable challenge was dislocating my patellar tendon in the middle of winter, which took me out of skiing and part of basketball season. It wasn't a long chapter, but looking back, I'm thankful. It gave me a gradual transition from elementary to high school, where everything starts changing quickly.

High school was full of fun, new experiences, and big shifts in people, some for the better, some not so much. I started playing high school football as a 14-year-old freshman, which was an eye-opener. We were practicing alongside 18-year-old seniors who had been training and lifting for years. I played quarterback, so I had a little protection during practice, but that didn't stop the seniors from taking a few hard shots at me. I had never been hit so hard in my life. We had a good year as a team, and when the season ended, I looked forward to baseball. Once again, it was a challenge hitting against seniors who were bigger, stronger, and threw harder, but it was another solid season. The rest of high school followed that pattern, football in the fall, baseball in the spring and summer, then repeat.

What changed the most was the people around me. I saw some friends dedicate themselves to getting bigger and stronger, some even turning to performance enhancers. I also saw others drift into the wrong crowd and start drinking and using drugs. Thankfully, most of my closest friends didn't go down either of those paths, but it was eye-opening to watch how quickly people could change. High school came with its share of normal fights and disagreements. One friend even got run over by a car, he turned out okay, but it was still just part of what ended up being a very full four years.

After high school, things got more interesting. I chose to play baseball in college and started at a junior college in western Kansas. I learned a lot, not just about the game, but about myself and other people. I learned how important human connection really is. My first roommate was a guy from my high school who was also on the team. His college career didn't last long. He was expelled for reasons that followed him from high school. I was moved into a new room with the tight end from the football team, a massive guy who made me look tiny. We actually got along great and found common ground, especially in our love for the outdoors.

When I returned for my sophomore year, I didn't know who I'd be rooming with. I ended up with a defensive tackle, another giant. But again, we clicked, found shared interests, and had a good year. Those two years taught me a lot about communication and how to get along with people from all different backgrounds. They also opened my eyes to the difference in talent between high school and college athletes. No matter how much people told me about the gap, seeing it first hand was something else.

Fortunately, I was able to continue my baseball career and transferred to a four-year college in South Carolina. That's when things really shifted. Our baseball team had about thirty-five guys, from twenty-five different states. Florida, New York, California, the Midwest, you name it. The level of talent was unreal. I realized quickly that I wouldn't be playing baseball after graduation. I got to watch athletes do things I didn't even think were possible, and they did them every day.

Up to this point, my life had been pretty smooth. But I learned in one night how fast everything can change. They say cats have nine lives, and if that's true, I'm sitting here today with about seven left.

During my junior year, a group of us decided to drive twenty minutes to a neighboring town for a night out. Four of us piled into a friend's pickup, two in the cab, and me and another guy lying down in the bed. Halfway through the drive, the truck started to swerve. My friend and I in the back had no idea what was happening since we couldn't see anything. I sat up to look through the windshield, and just then, the truck jerked back the other way. I was launched out of the truck, hitting the pavement at 50 miles per hour. The truck rolled onto its side. Thankfully, all my friends were okay. They started searching for me, expecting the worst. It took them twenty minutes to find me. I was sitting in a ditch, bloodied but alive.

They told me I was talking like nothing had happened, although I have no memory of it due to a concussion. The next thing I remember is waking up in the hospital, surrounded by doctors. I later found out just how close I came to not being here. I had fractured the back of my skull in two places. The lower fracture missed my spine by a hair. The upper fracture stopped just before my ear drums. Looking back now, I am beyond grateful to still be here and to see the sunrise each day.

More on the second time something happened in a bit.

In January 2020, I began focusing more on my health. I was eating better, walking every day, and feeling stronger mentally and physically. It was as if something inside me had woken up. I was more alert, more observant, and more curious about how my habits and choices could impact others. I knew I wasn't the only one going through the shifts that come with aging and wanting more from life.

The more I walked, the more alive I felt. Over time, my health improved dramatically. Like most people, I hit a plateau and started thinking about what more I could do. On September 19, I decided to stop drinking alcohol. It wasn't a dramatic declaration, I just wanted to take a break. I figured I'd only have a drink now and then for holidays or celebrations. But as those days came and went, I didn't go back. I still went out, still had fun, but I loved waking up clear-headed and energized. By January 2021, I made it official. I wasn't missing anything. Life was better without it.

Around midyear, I saw a sign-up for a 10K at Red Rocks Amphitheatre. I had never run a race before, but I decided to go for it. I started running instead of walking and made changes to my diet to get in better shape. I pushed myself hard. But I didn't balance the diet change well. The increase in protein and the intensity of training took a toll.

On September 1, 2021, while at home waiting for my daughter to get dressed for school, I had a seizure. She found me and called 911. I was taken to the hospital and placed in a medically induced coma for eight and a half days. Doctors told my parents multiple times they didn't know if I would pull through. Eventually, I did. I woke up with my mind coming back online, but my body was still struggling. I couldn't talk, and my motor skills were weak. But I started to recover. I was released from the hospital fourteen days after being admitted.

Once I got home and returned to daily life, I realized the race was still coming up. I told my friends and family I was still going to run it, which was met with understandable concern. I started walking again. My breathing recovered quickly, but my legs were slow to return.

For those who haven't been to Red Rocks, it's not flat. The course is filled with steep climbs and descents, and somehow it feels like more up than down. I didn't care about the time, I just wanted to finish. The 10K took me an hour and 45 minutes. For context, the winner finished an hour and 11 minutes ahead of me. But I finished. I ran it, forty days after a seizure and coma.

I still walk and hike every single day. I'm more active than ever. And I haven't even thought about drinking since September 19, 2020. I love my life more now than I ever have.

This isn't a chapter about running, eating clean, or quitting drinking. It's just the path I took. I wake up and go to bed each day grateful for every person and every experience in my life. I believe we all have two superpowers that can take us anywhere we want to go. Dedication and consistency. Be crystal clear about where you want to go and work each day toward that goal.

Do Different Now, ask yourself:

What shaped your life and decisions as an adult?

Chapter 2

Mindset

We are all told at different times throughout our lives to have a growth mindset, to make progress, to be mindful of who we surround ourselves with, the groups we associate with, and how we view each obstacle. There are a thousand different quotes and thoughts along these lines, and a ton of coaches and teachers who add their own perspective. What it boils down to in the end is this: what does it mean to you? I could speak to a group of 1,000 people and have 1,000 different meanings.

For me, it started with a deep look into myself and what I had become, the life I was leading, what it would look like if I stayed on that path, and what I truly wanted my life to look like. It was the difference between what I had become and what I wanted that led to my breakthrough.

I spent the majority of my career in new home sales. It was profitable and gave me a couple of weekdays off, but I also spent my weekends sitting in a garage with a few other salespeople, going through appointments and dealing with clients and prospects. As the years went on, my kids were getting older and becoming increasingly more talented at baseball and softball. With that talent came the opportunities to play with travel teams and fly around the country to participate in tournaments and be seen by more and more recruiters.

As the summers passed, I found myself more and more often watching their games on a very basic app, no video or sound, just dots moving around a diamond. My parents were great and would send videos when they could, but I was still missing out on those moments of youth and development.

I remember the day everything changed. It was a sunny Saturday in July, and both my kids were playing in tournaments. I was sitting in that same garage with three other salespeople. We were all between appointments. It had become my norm, being in that garage, selling homes, talking to clients, and being away from my children while they were doing something they loved.

That day, I was watching the dots move for my son's game. He was at bat. The dot made its way all around the bases, and then the caption popped up: "Home run,

Baker." In that moment, everything shifted. My mindset, my goals, my aspirations, what I wanted out of my life, and the legacy I wanted to leave behind. I spent the rest of the day reflecting on those questions, where I was, where I wanted to go, and what it would take to get there.

When I got home, I took a hard look in the mirror. I thought about what my relationship with my kids would look like if I stayed on the same path. The answer was clear. I wanted something different, so I decided to do something different.

I woke up on Sunday feeling renewed and invigorated. I had finally made the decision to take control of my life and my future. That morning, I walked into the garage and told my boss I was leaving. He laughed a little and told me to take the day off if I needed it. I said no, and handed in my keys. He still wasn't convinced. "OK," he said, "see you tomorrow." I looked at him and said, "No, you won't." Then I walked out the door.

Fortunately, I had already completed about 90 percent of my real estate license. It only took me a week to finish the coursework and take the tests. I passed. I was officially in business for myself. Most importantly, I could now control my schedule. I never had to watch the dots on my phone again.

At the time, I didn't know it, but that was just the first step in creating the life I wanted for myself and my kids. I still had to work harder than ever, because everything depended on me. But I also had the time and availability to be there, to share in the memories my kids were making with their friends and teams. Our relationship improved dramatically. And this was only the beginning of taking full ownership of my life. More on that later.

People love to talk about having a growth mindset, but what does that really mean? If you asked 100 people, you'd get 100 different answers. And that's OK. Growth is personal. There is no right or wrong definition. But to give yourself the best chance at making your dreams a reality, there are a few questions you need to ask yourself before setting any goals.

The first question is, how optimistic are you about your future? Do you believe your story is already written? That you'll never live your best life? That something will always come along to set you back? Or are you optimistic? Do you believe you'll either succeed or learn, even if you fall short? Will you persevere, no matter what challenges lie ahead? Is the life you desire out there, waiting for you to take action?

When facing a challenge or obstacle, where does your mind go first? Do you focus on the possibilities and what will happen when you succeed? Or do you begin looking for excuses, reasons it won't work, people or circumstances that will stand in your way? Do you search for the positive or the negative in each situation? Are you looking for opportunities or are you too distracted to notice the ones right in front of you?

If you set a goal and come up short, what is your response? Do you call it another failure and question why you even tried? Or do you treat it as an opportunity to learn? What went wrong? What can you do differently next time? Do you point fingers, or do you look at your plan, your effort, your follow-through? Your goals and your dreams belong to you, and you are 100 percent responsible for them.

Do you see people who are succeeding and assume it's just luck? Do you think everything must have been handed to them? Or do you look deeper? Do you ask what they've done to create that success? It's important to remember that most people only post their success on social media. They rarely show the 90 percent of the effort it took to get there. The overwhelming majority of people succeeding in life, in relationships, in health, and on purpose got there through planning, consistency, discipline, and a willingness to do the work.

Yes, some luck is involved. But the harder you work, and the more intentional your efforts, the more often good fortune finds you.

You also need to take stock of what's already going right. Too many people believe their lives are terrible and that nothing ever works out for them. That is simply not true. Every one of us has things, right now today, that are going right. It's more than just gratitude. It's acknowledgment.

Are you employed? Do you have friends? Family? A roof over your head? Do you realize that your dreams and aspirations are within reach? No matter where you are starting from, take a moment to list what's working. You'll be surprised at how long that list becomes. That's called progress.

You do not need to jump from zero to one hundred overnight. Focus on being just one percent better today than you were yesterday. That may sound small, but small steps lead to big change. Over the course of a year, or two, or five, imagine what your life would look like if you were one percent better every single day. That's 1,825 percent better after five years. Who wouldn't call that progress and success?

You have greatness inside you, find it, focus on it and use it.

When faced with anything new, a project, a goal, an obstacle, or a relationship, how do you view it and approach it? Does it make you feel uneasy? Do you look for reasons it can't or won't happen? Do you start thinking about the people who will prevent you from achieving what you set out to do? Do you make up a list of excuses or circumstances to blame even before you start?

Or, when approached with something new, do you feel excitement about doing something different? Do you look forward to figuring out how to make it work? And when challenges come up, do you start finding alternative paths and keep pushing forward? Life presents us with opportunities almost daily to do or try something new. A lot of our success or learning comes from how we feel about and approach these opportunities.

You can doom yourself before you even begin just by your thoughts and feelings. But the opposite is also true. You can increase your chances of success dramatically by approaching each new opportunity with a mindset focused on how to make it happen. This doesn't mean you have to be a risk-taker. It just means you recognize opportunities when they come and give thought to how you could make them work and what would happen if they did. Don't view opportunities as unachievable or out of reach, or immediately start looking for excuses as to why they wouldn't work.

Along with new opportunities, how often and how deeply do you dwell on past experiences? Do you think about them so deeply that they've paralyzed you from moving forward on anything new? When you think about past experiences, no matter the circumstances, do you immediately focus on all the bad things and how they hurt you, and then use those events as an excuse for the life you're living now?

Or is the opposite true? Do you look back at those past experiences and ask what you did or what you could have learned from them? I'm not saying we shouldn't remember our past. We need to learn from it so we can avoid similar mistakes or have an alternative path ready when something similar comes up again. This mindset takes discipline. There are things in every one of our pasts that were extremely painful, physically, emotionally, mentally, or spiritually.

Start with one memory that keeps showing up. Think about what happened. Think about how it impacted you. Then ask yourself if there was anything you could have done to change the outcome. If there were things you could have done, why didn't you do them at the time? What prevented you? What are you thinking now that you weren't thinking then? And most importantly, how will you recognize when something similar presents itself again, and what will your game plan be? Will you follow through with it?

Most people say that when you start something, a project, a challenge, a goal, you either succeed or you fail. I completely disagree. I don't think failure is ever an option. I believe you either succeed or you learn.

Thomas Edison is a perfect example. He tried tens of thousands of times to invent the lightbulb and finally succeeded. When asked why he kept going after so many failed attempts, he said he didn't fail once. He just found thousands of ways not to make a lightbulb. That is the mindset you want. Always be learning from success and especially when you fall short. When your mindset shifts toward learning, your outlook changes. You'll spend less time making excuses and more time finding better solutions.

We are all surrounded by people on a daily basis. Some are friends, some are family, and some are just faces in the crowd. One thing to be ready for when you decide to do something different is feedback and criticism from others. Some of it will be good, some neutral, but a lot of it will be questions and doubts, why are you doing what you're doing?

There are three types of people you'll encounter when you begin something new, especially when it involves self-improvement or a new direction in life.

The first group is your cheerleaders. These are the people who will join you. They see what you're doing, and you inspire them to make changes in their own lives. Their goals may be different, but they'll want progress too. They'll celebrate your wins and support you when you need encouragement.

The second type of cheerleader won't join you, but they'll cheer you on. They'll support your journey, but they are not willing or able to make any changes themselves. You need to be cautious with this group because they can quickly shift into critics. They're like fairweather friends, happy when things are going well but quick to doubt or question you when things get tough. I'm not saying you shouldn't have these people around. Just be aware of how they respond depending on your progress.

The third group is the anchor. These people not only won't join you, they'll actively try to hold you back. They're comfortable with the way things have been and with who you were before. They may say they're happy for you, but behind the scenes they'll question everything. They don't desire more out of life, and they don't want you to desire more either. They'll gossip, criticize, and try to keep the status quo.

You have two choices when it comes to this group. First, you can talk to them. Let them know what you're doing and why. Tell them this path comes with a new attitude and new behaviors. The second choice is to cut them loose. If they constantly speak negatively or try to pull you back into patterns that no longer align with your goals, you owe it to yourself and your aspirations to release them.

Here's what usually happens. The moment you let go of someone who no longer supports your growth, someone new will appear, someone who becomes a huge supporter and helps push you forward.

The last piece of mindset is looking at your confidence and self-worth. Take a moment to check in with yourself. This is a look in the mirror. There is no wrong answer. It's just an honest assessment of where you are now and what might need improvement.

If you're lacking in either area, create a game plan before diving into your goals. That way, you're starting with a strong foundation and giving yourself every chance for success. Rate where you are on a scale of one to ten. Do that every couple of weeks. You'll be amazed by the progress you see.

Here are a few tips to boost self-worth: prioritize self-care. Read. Educate yourself. Give yourself situations and observe how you react. Was your reaction thoughtful? Did it move you closer to your goals or further away?

One of the most overlooked practices is simply looking around. Notice the moments happening all around you, the sounds, the smells, the movement of the world and everyone in it. The biggest benefit is slowing down. The world moves fast, and everything tends to fly by. But when you focus your attention on the small things and allow yourself to be present, life slows down. You get space to think. Your plans become clearer. Your vision sharpens.

Reading is another simple but powerful tool. It doesn't have to be self-help or motivation. Read something you enjoy. Let yourself get lost in a story or another person's perspective. Dedicate just ten minutes a day.

Read in the morning, before bed, or during a break. That small act opens your mind. It gets you thinking in new ways. That is growth.

Finally, put yourself in a new situation, or revisit an old one, and pay attention to your first reaction. Do you go to a negative place and start listing excuses? Or do you see it as a learning opportunity? It's in those moments, and how you respond, that real growth happens. That's how you make progress, every day. That's how you level up your life.

In the end, getting into the right mindset before you start moving forward gives you the best shot at success. It helps you learn more about who you are, what you want, what you're willing to do, and how you've handled challenges before. And if you've never focused on mindset before, this is your moment to begin.

If you want different, do different.

This mantra is where your journey starts.

Have you ever told yourself this is your year, or now is your time, only to watch the opportunity slip by with no progress? Why did that happen? Was it an external factor? Were you too busy? Or was it really not the right time?

Here's the truth. Your thoughts and desires were probably real, but your effort was exactly the same as the last time you said it. You did the same things again, but expected a different result. That's not how it works.

If you've been getting the same results and don't change your approach, you are going to keep saying the same thing every single year. "This is my year." "It'll be different this time."

It won't be. Not unless you change how you go about creating that future.

If you want different, do different.

Do Different Now, ask yourself:

What prompted your desire for something different? Are you ready for growth?

Chapter 3

Purpose & Clarity

This may seem easy and straightforward, but it takes a lot of self-reflection and honesty to understand what has held you back in the past and why this time will be different. Let's start with purpose.

Do you do things intentionally, or react to them as the day comes at you? When you wake each morning, do you have goals or a target for what you will accomplish that day? You can ask a hundred people to define purpose and you will likely get a hundred different answers. Even deeper, if you ask those same people what their purpose is, most will not know or will give a very broad answer like getting through work without getting yelled at, or meeting friends for drinks and the game on Friday night.

There is nothing wrong with any of these answers or lack thereof, but you want more. Your vision is bigger than just those things right in front of you. Have intention and purpose for each moment and each decision in your day. Be specific. If something comes at you that does not move your life closer to your goals, how much effort and dedication should you give it?

Now, I am not naive. I realize most people have jobs with bosses and deadlines and projects. But are those your goals for your lifetime, or are they a means to get there? We all have things that require our attention each day to remain employed or to stay in people's good graces, but those items can be different from what we truly aspire to in order to live our best life.

Having an intention and purpose that drives us each day is progress. It allows us to improve by one percent every day. We have all heard it before, write down your obituary. What do you want people to remember you for, and what do you want them to say about you? I view it a bit differently. Don't write your obituary. Instead, write your legacy.

What do you want to leave behind when you are gone? How do your kids go about their lives? How did you impact the lives of your friends, your family, or even complete strangers? The biggest difference is this: your obituary is what people say and feel about you. Your legacy is what people tell and teach others about what being associated with you meant to their lives.

If you have a morning or nightly ritual, I do, though I'm not saying you have to, but it is important to start your day with intention and purpose. What do you want to accomplish for yourself that day? It could be something small, something that seems minor. But if it's your purpose, you'll make sure it gets done instead of pushing it off to tomorrow, then the next day, then forgetting it completely.

We have all experienced a lack of clarity in our lives, when everything around us is moving a million miles an hour, and everyone wants our time, energy, and attention. It feels out of control. That chaos takes away from our goals, our purpose, and our intentions for each day.

Gaining clarity in our lives is not easy. It takes effort. But clarity comes from stepping back, not adding more. If you have a project or a goal that you initially think will take ten steps, see what you can combine or cut to get it down to seven or eight.

Clarity helps in a few key ways. First, it simplifies your life. The world slows down when you aren't trying to complete an endless to-do list. Second, clarity removes the fog from your vision. It helps you focus on the most important actions, the ones that move your life forward. Clarity also creates space to focus on your own growth and development, especially when combined with a daily sense of purpose.

We've all seen programs or projects that come with a twenty-page workbook or detailed instructions. Be honest. When you see something like that, what is the first thing you feel? My guess is your eyes roll, maybe a groan, or a thought like, "What is this?" Does it give you clarity or confusion? Does it make you more or less motivated to follow through on the goal or project? Do you find yourself flipping pages, wasting time figuring out where you are or what's next?

We all know there are steps required to accomplish anything, but most times they can be simplified. You can combine steps and make the process cleaner and more effective.

The same idea applies to your lifetime goals and everything you hope to achieve. Yes, we know we can't go from where we are today to our best life in one step. But don't over complicate your focus. Keep your eye on where you want to go and why. Simplify the steps to get there. This allows your effort to go into the actual work, not figuring out what step you're on.

In the end, start your day with purpose. Be intentional with your energy and your efforts. This will lead to greater clarity. Without the chaos surrounding you, you'll be able to focus on what matters and make steady progress toward your goals.

Your clarity starts with being very specific about where you're going. It means removing distractions, setting aside excuses, and staying on your path. Your purpose is about being intentional. It's taking steps, even small ones, every single day. It's about having a defined plan from the moment you wake up to the moment you fall asleep.

Don't repeat the same efforts you've made in the past that didn't work. If it didn't work before, chances are it won't work now. Do something different. Be clear and intentional.

Do Different Now, ask yourself:

Do you have a purpose each day? Are you clear on what you desire and why?

Chapter 4

Inspiration

There is a definite difference between motivation and inspiration. Motivation is an external factor and can be fleeting. It can depend on your mood or what you see or how it speaks to you. We have all received or subscribed to a motivational quote or image of the day or have a calendar that is supposed to fire us up. I had those for the longest time, and it took one moment for me to realize that I needed something different.

I can still recall that moment as if it was yesterday. I woke up and looked at my phone for my motivation of the day. It was an amazing picture of a person in Norway, and they were a couple thousand feet up on a gorge overlooking this incredibly blue lake. There was a boulder that stuck out from the wall and the person had their arms raised. There was a quote on it, one I can't even remember. I probably didn't even look at it. The reason being, I'm afraid of falling. As soon as I saw the picture, I wasn't motivated at all. Quite the opposite. I felt fear, as if I was the one standing on the edge of that cliff.

Things like that can motivate people, but not everyone, especially when fear or other internal reactions get in the way. What fires one person up may not do the same for another. Motivation is temporary and often tied to outside circumstances. That is where the biggest difference lies between motivation and inspiration.

Inspiration is internal. It is unique to each of us. It is the why behind what we do and what drives us to want more. Thankfully, there is a simple way to find your true inspiration. As every fifth grade English teacher taught us, ask why at least five times to get to the real answer.

For me, I started with a weight loss goal, but it ended up being so much more than that. It still drives me today. It became nothing about the number on the scale. I found that by continually asking myself why it was important to hit my goal, who it was important to, and what I truly wanted, I uncovered the fire deep inside. That fire is still the biggest reason I do what I do every single day.

For me, the answer was my kids. I wanted to be active with them in life, not stuck on the sidelines because I wasn't healthy enough to join them. I didn't want to be the father who just watched. I wanted to be the father who, if they came home and said they wanted to go camping, hiking or skiing, wouldn't just hand them money or send them off, but would grab our gear, get in the truck, and go with them.

What started as a weight loss goal became a goal to be strong and active enough to share in these experiences with them. That goal has shifted and grown as they get older and I set new challenges for myself, but they are still at the heart of why I do what I do.

I want to leave my kids a legacy they can be proud of. Not money or things, but memories. Memories of the time we spent together and what we got to do. More than that, I want them to know the impact I had on other people. I want them to hear stories from those I coached and worked with, people who say their lives improved because of something I shared or helped them discover. I want my kids to have every opportunity in life, and to see the world and everything it holds, not just what is close to home. Like I said, they are my inspiration. They are what drives me to be one percent better every single day.

For all of us, it is important not to rely only on motivation to fuel us. It is more powerful to find our own inspiration. One of the easiest ways to do that is to start with your biggest life goal and ask yourself why it is important. Yes, you can still look for motivation in your surroundings, but that can't be the only thing that drives you. You have to reignite that fire that already lives deep inside you and use it as your fuel.

Be intentional. Ask yourself why, and don't do it just to check a box. Search for the truth behind why something is important to you, to your future, and to your goals.

Find inspiration in doing things differently this time around, and love the new journey. Appreciate when you do something you've never done before and it works. And if it doesn't work, appreciate that you learned something and now get to try again with something different. You will enjoy doing things differently just as much when you reach your ultimate goal or aspiration.

Do Different Now, ask yourself:

What inspires you?

Chapter 5

Importance of Ritual

At first glance, this may seem like I'm saying to repeat every day, which might sound like the opposite of what we've talked about so far, but it's not. In fact, it's the exact opposite.

The most successful people in the world, not just financially but in all areas of life, have two major things in common: dedication and consistency. When they set their sights on accomplishing something, they dedicate the time, effort, and focus to make it happen. Their goal becomes consuming, and it's what drives them each and every day. They are also consistent in their efforts. It's often said that it takes twenty-one days to build a habit. By making your goals your daily focus, the process of achieving them becomes a habit too.

Here's something important to remember: inaction can also become a habit. If you find yourself feeling like every day is the same, and you aren't fulfilling your goals or aspirations, chances are you've built a habit out of non-action. That pattern has become your normal, and it's time to break it.

Once you've established what your best life looks like and created a plan to get there from where you are now, begin with one thing you commit to fully, completely. Make it a non-negotiable in your life. Something you will do without fail, no matter what. Remember, you're not leaping over mountains in a single bound. The goal is to improve just one percent every day. And trust me, after a month, six months, or a year, you won't even recognize the person you started out as.

Think about the small things you can do to support your path. Is it how you wake up in the morning? When you get up? What you do at night before going to sleep? How are you ending your day in a way that puts you in the most positive position for tomorrow?

For me, I have both a morning and night ritual. It starts the moment I wake up. Before my feet even hit the floor, I spend a few minutes thinking about what's going right in my life, my business, my personal relationships, or the impact I'm having on others. I also set my focus on how I'm going to improve just one percent that day. There are a few other parts to it, but this ritual is personal to me.

That's the key. This ritual has to be personal to you. If a ritual isn't helping you succeed, don't do it. This is your journey, and your practice needs to put you in a position to grow each day.

At night, I have a similar, not identical, ritual before I go to sleep. Living your best life and setting meaningful goals requires both dedication and effort. Know this going in: there's no quick fix, no snap-your-fingers solution, no cheat code.

I could speak to a room of 1,000 people about what it means to live your best life, and every one of them would have a different path to get there. What works and what doesn't will be different and unique for each of them. That's because we are all different, and even our definition of what "living your best life" looks like is unique.

What is most important is developing a method you use daily that moves you closer to your goal and is straight-forward and repeatable.

Your daily ritual should be different than what you've typically done. If you've never been a morning person and have always stayed up late, switch it up. Get up early. Knock out breakfast, a workout, a shower, maybe even get some work done or set your schedule before anyone else is even awake. Getting things knocked out before others are even moving is a win in itself. It gives you a powerful feeling of having a head start, not just on your day, but on most of the world.

Also, try putting your electronics down by 9:30 and being in bed by 10:00. That gives your body and your mind time to decompress and get ready to do it again the next day.

This is how I structure my life and my days. These are just suggestions. They work for me, but they may not be right for you. If they aren't, find a daily structure that does. One that gives you wins and the opportunity to get things done when others aren't.

Most importantly, it has to be something that works for you and is repeatable every single day. Make it a ritual that becomes non-negotiable as part of the new version of yourself.

Do Different Now, ask yourself:

How would your life change if you dedicate time and effort toward what you desire?

Chapter 6

No Such Thing as Failure

Thomas Edison echoed this the best when he finally designed the lightbulb that worked. He was asked how he was able to keep going after failing so many thousands of times. He responded simply by saying he didn't fail once, he just learned thousands of different ways not to invent the lightbulb. We should all take this mentality to heart and make it part of how we approach anything.

When faced with a challenge, a goal, or something you aspire to, there are only two possible outcomes. You either succeed or you learn. In your history, you may have been taught about failure, and that kind of thinking often leads to giving up or giving in and settling for things the way they have been. It may have led you to avoid doing anything new or different or to hold back from striving to truly live your best life because of the fear of failing or falling short. Your past behavior might have taught you that when something doesn't work out, you shouldn't have done it in the first place.

This kind of thinking leads to a life of complacency. It makes you blend into the crowd. It causes you to make excuses, even before you get started, as to why it won't work. You may blame time, other responsibilities, friends, family, work, or any number of other things. You justify them as reasons, but let's be honest, they are not reasons. They are excuses. You are trying to protect yourself and your mindset from doing anything that has a risk of not going exactly the way you planned. But if you continue thinking that way, you are choosing to live an ordinary life. You are choosing to stay with the crowd that is not daring to achieve more.

Before you start writing or planning or getting going on your goals, you have to work on your mindset first. Build a strong foundation to give yourself every and best opportunity to achieve what you set out to. There are a lot of things you can do, as discussed in an earlier chapter, but one of the biggest things you can do is develop a learning mindset. Take every opportunity and situation to learn from. That could be from yourself and your history, others in your life, social media, seminars you have gone to, and more. Each of them offers an opportunity to learn and add to the skills you already have and utilize.

Remember, there is no such thing as failure, just opportunities to learn, adjust, and keep going. When you get to the point where you are tired of living an ordinary life and desire more, start with your history. Why is this time the one that you will see through? What makes it different now? What has prevented you from doing something in the past, or if you have started a plan but did not achieve what you desired, what happened? What came up that derailed you from moving forward or making an adjustment, and although the path was different, you still had the clarity of your ultimate goal? Take a second look at your history, but instead of looking at the excuses or justifying that the time was not right, learn from them. What did they teach you, and how are you going to do things differently this time around? It is vitally important not just to set your goals for your lifetime but also look at what held you up with prior goals or what may present itself this time around. Don't just think about them, come up with a game plan for how you will adjust when those times or feelings show up again, because they will.

Do not live a life and end up with regrets of things you didn't do, opportunities you didn't take advantage of, relationships you didn't take the time or opportunity to develop. Time keeps going, there is no stopping it. At the same time, it is there for each and every one of us to take advantage of the moments we are presented with, shown, or find on our own. You will be absolutely amazed when you develop a growth and learning mindset and failure is no longer an option for you. You will begin to notice how many different opportunities show up and how many you actually see. Time will not stop, but it will slow down because you will begin to see and appreciate all the moments that surround each of us every day.

Life and goals and aspirations are not a pass or fail test. It is to achieve or learn and adjust. There is way more than one answer in life, and if you approach it as opportunities to learn, you will find the best way for you as a unique individual to make it happen.

Learning is a lifelong journey. Every angle, moment, day, and situation offer opportunities for each of us to discover new things about ourselves. Don't let them slip through your fingers. Take advantage of them to discover what may work or not work for you. Different things and methods work for each of us as individuals. What one person may have success with, another may not. You won't know what method or mentality will work for you unless you learn from others' success or challenges. Approach each interaction with curiosity and wanting to know more about yourself.

Remember, there is no such thing as failure, only opportunities to learn. Using Edison as the example, how often do you think he made the lightbulb the same way as before if it didn't work? The adjustments may have been extremely small, but they were different based on what he had learned up to that point. He desired to design the lightbulb, and each time he didn't, he adjusted and did something different.

Take this lesson when you are designing the future, new, and better version of yourself. Learn from the efforts in your past, what worked and what didn't, and then do something different to attain something different.

Do Different Now, ask yourself:

Looking back and now forward, how will you approach each challenge to either succeed or learn?

Chapter 7

Grow, Every Single Day in Every Possible Way

It may seem like a small or even insignificant goal, but your aim should be to improve yourself by one percent every single day. It sounds like such a small amount, but we need to stop comparing ourselves and our lives to what we see on social media or through friends and family. The focus has to be on improving ourselves. One percent a day may not feel like much, but imagine that improvement over a year, five years, or a decade. After ten years, that would mean you are 3,650 percent better than you are today. Would you take that? Would you even recognize the person you were when you started this journey?

Be intentional each day when you wake up. Set a clear focus for how you are going to get one percent better. Every decision you make, from how you start your morning to how you structure your time throughout the day, has the potential to move you forward. Each small decision could be the tipping point between making progress and staying stuck. Being intentional takes effort, and it takes planning. Over time, it becomes part of who you are when faced with any decision.

Intentional living begins with knowing the outcome you desire. Ask how the question, project, or challenge in front of you will help you get there and then choose actions that move you closer. It starts with a pause. There is a real difference between reacting and responding. Most of us have witnessed arguments in public, at a bar, on the street, or in social situations, where people are reacting. There is no filter, no thought behind the words, just emotion and impulse. Those situations usually end in a fight, a breakup, or something no one planned for their night.

If you find yourself in a similar situation, whether at work, in your health journey, or in a relationship, take a moment to pause. Ask yourself what your intention is. What is the other person really saying? Once you've taken that moment to reflect, then respond with clarity. That pause is often what separates people who are progressing from those who stay stuck. Sometimes, the best response is no response. Choosing silence and walking away can be the most powerful decision you make. That level of awareness shows real growth and confidence in who you are becoming.

Opportunities for growth show up every day, often more than once. We all know people who seem to always be working on something new, connected to everything, and moving forward with purpose. What do you think about those people? Do you believe they're just lucky? Do you assume everything was handed to them? Or do you recognize the behind-the-scenes effort they've put in to get where they are?

Look closer. These are people who have been intentional about their growth. They've worked hard in private, created momentum, and positioned themselves to take advantage of opportunities. People are drawn to them not because they are loud or flashy, but because there is something magnetic in their presence. They speak with purpose. They show genuine interest in others. Whether they are introverts or extroverts doesn't matter. Curiosity belongs to everyone.

Even if you consider yourself introverted, you can step into growth by listening, asking open-ended questions, and observing more deeply. Watch how others speak and respond. When asked a question, do they pause before answering? Chances are they do. They are thoughtful because they want their answer to address not just the question asked, but the one that comes next.

Slowing down, becoming curious, and watching how people and situations unfold around you is a powerful practice of personal growth. Every day, try to learn something new about yourself, about others, or about the environment you're in. When you share an opinion, ask for feedback. Listen fully to what people say. If they sense you are truly open to learning, they will be honest, even if they disagree. Their perspective might not match yours, but it can spark a deeper conversation.

If you've never done this before, or if it pushes you out of your comfort zone, good. That is where growth happens. You will not grow while staying comfortable. You grow by stretching. By trying something different. By pushing beyond what you once thought were your limits. You may not get it right the first time. It might feel awkward. That is not failure, it's part of learning. The key is to keep going. Keep learning. Keep pushing forward.

There is also a health aspect to personal growth. That one percent each day includes your body. It doesn't mean spending hours in the gym or hiring a personal trainer. It can be as simple as paying attention to what you eat and making time for daily movement. When I first started with the goal of being more active for my kids, I didn't do anything extreme. I made small adjustments in my diet and started walking. That was it. But I did it every day. Over time, it became a habit and remains one of the most important parts of my life.

As mentioned in a previous chapter, building ritual into your day is powerful. So why not make better eating and daily movement part of that ritual? It doesn't need to be complicated. Just make it consistent.

And when you hit your goals, celebrate. It doesn't have to be a big deal. When you accomplish something you set out to do, even something small, give yourself credit. If you use to-do lists, don't just cross items off or mark them with a red X. Instead, write something next to each one. Write "accomplished" or "crushed it." Those small moments of acknowledgment reinforce your commitment and give you a boost of pride. They add up.

In the end, every single day gives you a chance to grow in some way. Your job is to stay aware and prepare yourself mentally, physically, emotionally, and spiritually to take advantage of those chances. Growth means learning what works and what doesn't, paying attention to how you react and how you adjust. If you are committed to building a new version of yourself and a better future, know that challenges will come. Especially when you're doing things differently. That's okay. Expect them. Prepare for them.

The key is having a plan before you begin. That way, when a challenge shows up, you already know how you're going to handle it. You stay in motion. You keep making progress.

This journey will look different from what you've done before. That's part of the beauty of it. Testing yourself, exploring your comfort zone, and moving beyond it. You don't grow when you're comfortable. You grow when you are stretched. When you challenge your limits. When you make the decision to do things differently and see how far you can go.

Do Different Now, ask yourself:

How will you focus on daily growth?

Chapter 8

Realization

Your Initial Goal Was Too Small and Is Beneath You

This is one of the most enjoyable moments you will experience. When you begin crafting your lifetime goals, they will likely feel too big, out of reach, and far beyond anything you believe you can handle. You may feel like your eyes are bigger than your stomach. Then you start. You make progress. You begin to see the changes, and you feel the improvement in your life. You start to love the new version of yourself that you're creating. You keep showing up, pushing forward, and making strides. Then one day, it happens, you realize that what once felt like a lofty and far-off dream now feels small. The very goal you thought was your big breakthrough no longer seems big enough. From that moment, the sky is the limit. You adjust your vision. You stretch your identity. And you begin to realize that the life you're building wasn't even something you could have imagined when you started.

It doesn't take years to feel this shift. For a former client, Katie, it took just four weeks.

When we first met and talked about her goals, she was unsure if they were even possible. She is married and has three kids. As time had gone by and her kids grew older, she began to feel more and more detached from their lives. Her relationship with her husband didn't feel like it once had. It felt more like two roommates raising kids than a connected, loving couple. What she truly wanted was a deeper relationship with her kids, one where they shared life with her, talked about challenges, celebrated wins, and built lasting memories. With her husband, she wanted to return to the feeling they had when they first fell in love. She missed the desire, the romance, and the joy of simply enjoying one another's company. She wanted others to look at them and see the kind of relationship that made people believe in lasting love. She told me she wanted to dance in the kitchen with him while they cooked dinner, to laugh, to have fun, something that hadn't happened in at least ten years.

In her words, she wanted the kind of family relationships people dream about. She didn't want to aim for them. She wanted to live with them every single day.

At the beginning, she worried that wanting all of this was asking for too much. She had already begun to lower her goals before she'd even started. We talked through it and agreed, there was no point in setting goals that were anything less than what she truly wanted. Her desires mattered. They were possible. They were worth pursuing.

Her first step was to sit down with her entire family. She shared her heart and her vision. She told them what she wanted and why it was important, to stay close, to grow together, and to build something lasting. Her first suggestion was Sunday dinner. The whole family would cook together, including her husband. That first Sunday was a little awkward. Everyone wanted to support her, but they weren't sure what she really expected. During dinner, the conversation opened up. Each person started to share what they wanted and what they saw for the family. The night ended positively.

During the week, Katie made time to talk to each of her kids individually. These weren't talks about school or chores. They were conversations about life, stories, interests, and connection. She also committed to spending the last thirty minutes before bed with her husband, without electronics, just being together and reconnecting.

Each week, things got better. Her family started to respond. Each of them, one by one, thanked her for starting something new and asked how they could help. Katie still felt there was more to be done, but she wasn't slowing down. She knew they were moving in the right direction.

By week five, something shifted. She showed up to our call with a completely different energy. She was glowing. She was full of confidence and joy. She started the call by saying, "It happened." Her voice lit up the room. She shared that she and her husband had gone to a friend's house, and a couple of neighbors pulled her aside. They told her how proud they were of what she was doing and how her family looked like something out of a magazine. Then she said something that still gives me chills. She said, "When they told me that, the thought in my head was, you haven't seen anything yet."

That was the moment. She had passed her original goal. What once felt far away was now just a stepping stone to something bigger. She was energized. She was confident. Most importantly, she was happy. Her original goal had been met, and surpassed. Now she was expanding her vision.

Her family started to set their own goals too. They shared them with each other. They encouraged and supported one another. They held each other accountable. They were all growing together.

I cannot wait to see what's next for Katie and her family.

The lesson here is simple, don't limit yourself when setting your lifetime goals. They are meant to stretch you, not shrink you. They are goals for your lifetime, not your next month. Don't begin your journey by putting a ceiling on your potential. Ask yourself what your best life looks like and start from there without limitations. Your smaller, measurable goals will come later as you figure out the steps to get where you want to go.

If your dream is to travel the world, name that. If you want to start your own business and become your own boss, say so. It doesn't matter how big the dream is or what area of your life it's in. Don't shrink your goal just to make it feel more reasonable. You will face challenges. You will adjust. You will learn along the way. But you will never find out what you are truly capable of unless you aim high and build a plan to get there.

By choosing to be uncomfortable and doing things differently, Katie and her family achieved a life they never imagined. They created connection, laughter, and daily memories. They stepped into a new version of themselves. It started with a moment of reflection, looking at their actions and inactions, deciding they wanted something different, something better, and most importantly, putting it into action.

Words are just words until you back them with effort. Action is what turns intention into reality. Without it, there is no progress. Talking about change won't create it. Doing something different will.

Do Different Now, ask yourself:

What is your plan for what lies ahead when you surpass your initial goal?

Chapter 9

Simple, Not Easy

This may be the most important thing to understand if you want to achieve what you set out to do. Setting goals and building a process to reach them is simple. I designed it to be that way. But simple does not mean easy. It still requires effort, dedication, consistency, and the willingness to intentionally make yourself uncomfortable. That's where real growth happens.

There are countless things that will impede your vision. Distractions show up to cloud your clarity and make you lose sight of where you are going. These distractions can come in the form of friends, family, work, responsibilities, time, or setbacks that make you question whether it's even worth continuing.

The best way to stay on track is to keep your process simple. Don't create a thousand steps or overly complicated procedures with binders and worksheets before you're even allowed to move forward. Simplicity clears the fog and allows you to keep your goal front and center. It helps you focus on the progress you make each day.

Let's take a closer look at the difference between simple and easy. Simple means something is straightforward. It means the path is clear. Easy, on the other hand, means something doesn't take much effort. Creating a new version of your life will not be easy. It will challenge you in more ways than you expect. And that's a good thing. It means you're doing something that matters. It means you're growing.

If what you're doing isn't new to you, then ask yourself why it hasn't worked yet. If you keep getting stuck in the same place or for the same reasons, it's time to do something different. Think back to Edison. Do you think he made the lightbulb the same way each time, hoping it would finally work? Of course not. He built a version, tested it, studied what failed, and made an adjustment. Then he built again. Over and over until it worked. It wasn't easy, but it was simple. Build. Test. Learn. Adjust. Repeat. That mindset is what kept him moving toward a clear vision.

Simplicity doesn't just apply to your goals. It applies to your life.

There are things you can do to simplify when everything around you feels like it's moving at a thousand miles an hour. Start by prioritizing your time each day. When something comes up, take a moment to pause and ask yourself if it aligns with your goals and your intention for the day. Is this going to move you forward? Often, what feels urgent is just busy work, and when you look closely, it doesn't deserve all of your time.

Simplify your routines. If something takes ten steps, find a way to do it in five. When you do that consistently, your mental load lightens, and you have more capacity to focus on what really matters.

Figure out a time management system that works for you. There are plenty of them out there, time blocking, Eisenhower boxes, and many more. Spend a little time researching, then try one that fits how your mind works. The right system will help you simplify your schedule and make each day more productive and focused. Along with that, you have to learn how to set boundaries and say no. If you don't, you become the catch-all for everyone else's problems and priorities.

That may have been your old pattern, but it's not part of who you are becoming.

Build space into your day for breaks. Even five minutes of focused breathing or quiet reflection can reset your energy and help you re-center. Taking time for yourself during the day can reduce stress, increase clarity, and allow you to make better decisions.

Limiting distractions will give you time back in your day. How many conversations or meetings have you sat through that added nothing to your life or goals? Be honest about that. If you find yourself caught in something unproductive, excuse yourself politely and return to what matters. The same goes for the time you spend online. Set limits for social media and mindless scrolling. Give yourself a window of time and stick to it. These changes will give you hours back.

Again, this is time you have added to your day. With the changes you are putting in place, it's important to take a few minutes and reflect on what you're doing. Look at what worked and what didn't, then make adjustments. Notice I said what worked, not what made you uncomfortable. Putting yourself in uncomfortable situations is exactly where growth happens. If you tried a time management system and it just didn't work for you, that's fine. Look at what part of it worked and what part didn't. Then, the next day, do something different based on how it went. You're not starting over, you're building off what you've learned.

Simplify your relationships too. As you grow, you will naturally attract some people and lose others. That's part of it. If a relationship nourishes you, emotionally, mentally, or spiritually, keep it and allow it to grow. But if it is draining, negative, or filled with complexity that holds you back, it's time to let that relationship go. The space it leaves behind will create room for something better.

When you simplify your life and get crystal clear on where you're going, why you're going there, and how you're going to get there, you can start building a new version of yourself. Yes, the process is simple. But no, it will not be easy. And that's exactly how it should be. When you work for something, the reward means more.

Do you recognize the type of person who is always talking about what they're going to do in the future? They talk a lot, but they don't follow through. The excuses come quickly, blaming other people, time, bad luck, or a long list of external reasons. They rarely hold themselves accountable.

You are not that person anymore.

My challenge to you is this: stay quiet about the work you're doing. Let the results speak for themselves.

Do Different Now, ask yourself:

How will you make your goals and life simpler, knowing it will require work and dedication?

Chapter 10

If You Want Different, Do Different

It is such a simple saying, but it can be one of the hardest things for people to recognize and put into practice. How often have you said or heard others say, "This is my year," or "My time is now"? Why this year? Why now? Why hasn't it happened before? Did something actually change, or is it just another moment of motivation that feels different? Most of the time, nothing has changed at all. People believe that by saying it out loud, they will somehow manifest their best life into reality. They believe it is just their turn. Some think they are owed something or that a once-in-a-lifetime event, like winning the Powerball, will show up and change everything. That is a rare occurrence, and yet many people count on those things to shape their future. The truth is, if nothing changes, nothing changes.

There are many aspects of doing things differently to get different results, and a lot of it happens before you even start the work. First is your mindset. Do you have a growth attitude, and how do you approach challenges? Are you optimistic about your future, or do you feel like the world is against you? Do you believe something will always come up and block your progress? It's essential to focus on the positives in every situation instead of immediately identifying the negatives and talking yourself out of success.

When you face a setback or an obstacle, how do you respond? These situations should be treated as learning opportunities, not reasons to stop. Challenges are going to come up, especially when you're doing something new. No matter how well you plan or how dedicated you are, things will go sideways from time to time. How you handle those moments matters more than trying to avoid them altogether.

Are you in control of your own goals and aspirations, or are you waiting for someone or something else to come along and make your success happen? The more ownership you take, and the less you depend on outside forces, the better your chance of building the life you want. You become fully accountable for your goals, your effort, and the progress you make each day.

When you're presented with an opportunity to do something new, how do you approach it? Do you see it as a great experience and a chance to succeed or learn something valuable? Or do you shrink back because it makes you uncomfortable? You have to get comfortable being uncomfortable. That is where real growth takes place. Growth rarely happens when you're coasting through life. It happens when you're stretched, mentally, emotionally, and spiritually. And when you hit a milestone or achieve a goal, celebrate it. Even if the win feels small, let it feed your spirit. That success will feed your soul, and soon, you'll crave more.

Most importantly, if you want to do things differently, you have to look at what you've done in the past. Where did you succeed? Where did you fall short? What led to those results? This is something you must do before you start. Otherwise, you risk repeating the same patterns and ending up with the same results. And that's not what you want. You're not doing all this to stay stuck. You want different. You want more. You want to live an extraordinary life.

Take an honest look in the mirror. Think back to the last time you made a resolution or faced a challenge. Did you hit the goal? Did you quit? What happened? How did you approach it, and what might you do differently now? This is the kind of self-reflection that changes lives. Are you someone who takes ownership of your success, or do you start pointing fingers the moment things don't go as planned? There's only one person who controls your success or failure, and that's you.

You are in charge of setting your goals, creating the plan, showing up every day, and adjusting when things don't go as expected. No one else. Just you.

The lesson in this chapter is as simple as the phrase itself. If you want different, do different. It may sound cliché, but it's true. If you walk away from this book with just one takeaway, let it be this. Look at your past efforts. If you didn't get what you wanted, why not? Was there no plan? Did you think just getting started was enough? Did you come into it already thinking about what might go wrong or why it wouldn't work? Be honest. That's the first step toward doing different.

Setting goals and achieving them isn't a random act. It's not something that just happens. It takes clarity, intention, and a willingness to reflect on your past. It takes a shift in mindset and a new way of approaching opportunities. There's more to this journey than just what's written in this chapter, but if you start with this truth and build from it, you'll drastically improve your chances of creating your best life.

Do Different Now, ask yourself:

How will your approach be different, to get a different result?

Chapter 11

Bridge

When faced with one, will you cross it and say goodbye to your old life?

This provides such a powerful visual for doing something different and facing the challenges that come with it. You've lived a certain way up to this point and then comes the moment when you decide you want more. You want extraordinary. That moment, right there, is your bridge.

Let's start by looking at where you are now, or where you stay if you decide not to cross the bridge. The truth is, this is where at least ninety-five percent of people live, ordinary. They repeat the same routine day after day. They try setting goals or resolutions only to give up within a month. They blame their clothes, their job, their schedule. They wait for a lucky break, an inheritance, a promotion, a winning lottery ticket, that most likely will never come. These are the people you see every day at work, at social events, talking about plans that never change. There's nothing wrong with them, but that's not the life you want. You want more. You want extraordinary. You want to become the person others look at and say, "You're so lucky." But it's not luck. It's mindset, planning, and most of all, it's the effort you put in to earn that life. The reason you don't see those people as often is because they associate with others like them. They don't stand in the crowd, they've stepped beyond it. You may have thought their life was unattainable. But when you commit to doing different, people will look at you that way.

Take a good look at your week. What are you doing? How are you spending your time? What lights you up? If you're still living an ordinary life, I'll make a few guesses. Around halfway through Sunday, you start dreading Monday. You either spend the rest of the day stressing or you push it aside and pack your last bit of the weekend with errands, drinks, games, anything to distract you. Monday morning, the alarm goes off and feels cruel. You drag yourself out of bed and either head to an office or your desk at home. You spend the first half of Monday chatting, catching up, avoiding. Then you eat lunch, get a bit done, and watch the clock. You go home, maybe play with your kids, maybe just zone out with a show or your phone. Then it's dinner, more screen time, and bedtime with that same creeping dread for Tuesday. Then it all repeats, Tuesday through

Thursday. But Friday is different because it's almost the weekend. You wake up in a better mood, breeze through the morning trying to finish what didn't get done, take a long lunch, and by 3 p.m. you've checked out. Friday night and Saturday feel like your time again. You do what you want, maybe it's lunch with friends, dinner out, catching a game, or just relaxing because it's the weekend. Then Sunday shows up. The morning is good, maybe a nice breakfast, a round of golf or whatever's on your list. But by the afternoon, that all-too-familiar feeling creeps in. You realize the weekend is slipping away, and Monday's already knocking. The cycle is about to start all over again. Now repeat that 50 times a year. I'll even assume you actually take your vacation, even though 75% of you don't. Now relive those 50 weeks for 40 years. That's 2,000 weeks that look basically the same.

Does that sound familiar? That is ordinary. But it doesn't have to be your reality. You can face the bridge, cross it, and commit to living differently. To living extraordinarily. To create the life you aspire to, or thought was out of reach.

Every decision point in life is a bridge. And you always have a choice. You can choose not to act, which is still a choice, and keep living the way you have. Or you can decide to cross the bridge. If you do, make that decision fully. No hesitation. No second guessing. Step into it with everything you've got. Then, once you cross, burn that bridge. Commit to never going back to the old version of yourself. That visual is important because it symbolizes the end of excuses, the end of playing small, and the beginning of actual change.

There are two types of people when it comes to goals. The talkers and the doers. The talkers are everywhere. They say this is their year, or their time is coming. They have grand visions of what life will look like "someday." But when it doesn't happen, the excuses start. It was the timing, the people, the economy. It's never their fault. The truth is, nothing ever changes for them because they're waiting for perfect conditions. But the stars don't align on their own. And when the perfect opportunity does show up, they don't take advantage of it because they have trained themselves to protect their psyche and their safety. We see them every day, in every walk of life, talking and talking about some future event they're waiting on, the one thing that will finally flip the switch and let them start living their best life. Sadly, those dreams, aspirations, ideas, and opportunities never get acted on. They end up wasted and buried right along with them in the grave.

On the flip side, we all know people who don't talk much about what they're doing or what their life will look like once a bunch of things fall into place. They just make things happen. Repeatedly. These individuals are always ready to take advantage when something presents itself. They're the opposite of the talkers. They don't waste time describing what they're going to do, they just take action. When an opportunity shows up, they do a quick analysis of whether or not it benefits their goals, and if it does, they make a decision and move forward. No hesitation.

They've conditioned themselves through experience, mindset, and attitude. They know if they don't take action, nothing will happen and tomorrow will look just like yesterday. They face the same bridges as everyone else, but they cross them, burn them, and keep moving. And the more you watch them, the more you might be shocked by the opportunities they seem to get. A lot of the time, they aren't even looking, opportunities just seem to show up.

You may find yourself wondering how they're different, why things seem to come so easily for them. It's their attitude. When you decide to cross the bridge and start doing something different, the same kind of things will start happening to you. As you grow and make progress, you become an attractor. People are drawn to you. They may not even know why, but there's something about your energy, your focus, your progress, and they want to be a part of it.

The most successful people aren't superhuman. They're just like everyone else, but they've made a decision to deal with life differently. They handle the challenges, take the opportunities, and keep going. They've chosen to do different.

Do Different Now, ask yourself:

Are you a talker or a do'er?

What will it look like if you stop talking and start doing?

Chapter 12

Don't Have Dreams, Have Goals

We are all taught as kids to have big dreams and not let anything stand in our way. But as we get older, time, responsibilities, and circumstances show up, and suddenly we're making excuses for why we can't live the dream we once had in our minds. Most of the time, dreams are made up of things beyond our control magically happening, winning the lottery, becoming the perfect fit for someone, or being the only choice for a big promotion and raise. But how often have those things actually happened for you? And how likely are they to happen in your future?

Sure, buy a lottery ticket if you want, but don't make it part of your life plan.

If you close your eyes and think back to when you were nine years old, before the limitations of life took hold, what were those dreams? What would the nine-year-old version of you say about the life you're living today? Would they be proud and excited for you? Would they high-five you for chasing those childhood dreams? Or would they look at you with confusion and ask, "What are you doing?" Would they wonder why you haven't traveled, why you look or feel the way you do, or what happened to that excitement and passion for life?

Can you pinpoint the moment those dreams faded away? When you started living the same life, repeating the same weeks and days over and over again? If you see yourself in that cycle, here's the great news, it doesn't matter how old you are or how long you've been doing the same thing. You have the power to change it, starting right now.

The person you are destined to become is the person you decide to be. You have the power to change the trajectory of your life at any moment, for any reason. It doesn't depend on anyone else. Today can be the day you choose to restart and refocus.

And this is where the difference between dreams and goals really shows up. Dreams are what we all had when we were kids. Back then, we didn't know what life would require of us. We didn't understand the time, effort, and intentionality it would take to live our best life. But when you decide to take action, to do something different to create a new life, that's no longer a dream. That's the goal.

Goals are real. They're driven by clarity and defined by measurable steps, even if those steps are just the efforts you make each day. Be very intentional about what you want. Is it better health? More wealth? Deeper relationships? Get specific. Be honest. Start there. Then work backward. What needs to happen between now and the life you want? What steps need to be taken? What do you need to change? What's worked before that you can do again?

I'll be honest, this part can be difficult, especially if you're nowhere near where you want to be right now. It's going to take a lot of different actions, new behaviors, and effort you may not be used to. And yes, a lot of it will make you uncomfortable. But that's the best part. Growth only happens when we're uncomfortable. You just have to decide to keep going anyway.

Take a look at your past. What has stopped you from living your best life before? Be honest. Write those things down and make a game plan for what you'll do when they show up again, because they will. Most importantly, once you're clear on where you want to go, how to get there, and what's held you back before, it's time to take a hard look at yourself and your mindset. If you need to, go back and reread the chapter on mindset.

No matter when in your life you've picked up this book or found this message, it's not too late. Living the life of your dreams is what nine-year-olds think about, and now, you're doing it for real. You're living your life by design, on your terms, built on the goals you've laid out for yourself. And the more progress you make, the more opportunities will show up. There's a good chance you'll even look back one day and realize that the dream your nine-year-old self had was actually too small.

You're living a life according to your goals, because you made a choice. You decided you wanted something different than what you had, and you did something different to live an amazing life.

Do Different Now, ask yourself:

What will you do today to make your dreams for your future your goal?

Chapter 13

Go, NOW!

Tell me if you've heard this one before. You set a New Year's resolution, usually about health, wealth, or relationships, and declare that this is going to be your year. Within a couple of weeks, your plan goes off the rails. You miss a few days or lose momentum and suddenly you're not where you thought you'd be. That's when the excuses start, reasons you haven't done what you said you would. But let's be honest, they're not reasons. They're excuses, and they're your mind's way of protecting itself.

By the end of February, just like 99% of people, your resolution is already a thing of the past. You missed too much time, didn't see the results you hoped for, or got frustrated with how hard it felt. So you decide this wasn't your year after all, but next year will be. You make a quiet promise to yourself, and for a moment you feel fired up and committed. But guess what? The next year looks exactly the same. You haven't changed your approach. You haven't figured out how to deal with the obstacles that are bound to come up. So when they do, they derail you again. Sound familiar? Be honest, how many years has this been your story? And what have you done to get a different result?

Here's the best part: you have total control to break the cycle. You don't need to wait for the next year to get started. Why not start today? You already know there are parts of your life where you're not living the way you want to. So what's stopping you from doing something different right now?

Human beings tend to want a date or a time when they change from one thing to another, which explains New Year's resolutions. Old was last year, new is this year. But there's nothing out there that says noon can't be the old and 12:01 the new. The decision lies with each of us, to make the choice to do things differently, to create a new version of ourselves and a better future, and that can happen on April 25th. These are just dates on a calendar. This is your life. You control what you do, how you view things, and how you approach every single moment.

If you've had a rough morning on a Wednesday and step out to grab something to eat, you might be upset or frustrated with how the morning has gone. But you can change it over that meal. Don't let things dwell or build up. They're not likely to get better on their own, more often than not, they'll get worse unless you change something about them.

To summarize this chapter: don't be the person who always talks about what will happen when x, y, or z finally falls into place. Don't keep saying how next year will be your year. Take action now. Put this book down and think of something small you want in this moment, and then do something about it, right now. Get comfortable taking action instead of just talking about taking action someday.

There's no better time to do something different than the moment the thought first comes into your mind. That's when your thinking is clear, and your reason for wanting it is right there in front of you.

So, did you put the book down and take action?

Be honest. If not, why didn't you?

Do Different Now, ask yourself:

Have you taken action yet? Why not?

CHAPTER 14

CHALLENGES

When you decide that you want something different in your life or future, and what you've done in the past hasn't worked, so now you're going to do it differently, expect challenges. Some of them you'll recognize, things you've faced before with varying degrees of success. But because you're doing things differently this time, there will be new challenges too. You won't be able to predict every single one, but that's no excuse not to try. Think through as many as possible and come up with your game plan for how to adjust when they do show up.

That way, when a challenge presents itself, not only are you expecting it, but you already know how to handle it. You won't be derailed like before. Instead, you'll course correct and move forward. I'll walk you through a number of the most common challenges people face when they're crossing the bridge and creating a new version of themselves. Some will be unique to you, but this list should help you start making progress toward living your best life.

Some challenges will be internal, stuff you bring with you. Others will be external, from friends, family, your environment. Either way, they need to be considered. With external challenges, you may even need to remove certain people from your life. Let's start with the internal ones.

Lack of Clarity – You have not clearly identified what you want and the future version of yourself. The result is a lot of clouds and distractions getting in the way and adding confusion to your challenge. The best way to get your clarity is to define in detail exactly what you want, why you want it, and the impact it has on your future. Make it part of your morning ritual to define your day.

Lack of Motivation – You either struggle to get going or to maintain your momentum because you aren't feeling it, you're tired or you're not making the progress quick enough. Best guidance here is to stop relying on motivation and find your inspiration, which is the why behind what you are doing. Why is it important that you succeed and who else is it important to and what ignites that fire deep inside you that can't be extinguished? Finding your true inspiration and asking the why questions eliminate your dependency on motivation.

Fear of failure – No one likes to not succeed at what they set out to, but it is important to remember your mindset, which you worked on before even starting your path, there is no such thing as failure, only opportunities to learn. If there is something you are struggling to overcome, figure out why you are having the problem, make a course correction, and keep pushing forward.

Fear of Success – What will my friends think? How will my life change? Will people approve or will they not like me? This is a new version of yourself you are creating and making happen and not everyone will approve or understand, and that is fine. You know the benefits of doing this for yourself and those closest to you, and that is what matters the most. The people that don't approve or are not happy, let's face it, they lack the courage to make any changes themselves and their only way to handle it is to try and bring people back down to the level they are comfortable. Don't let them. You have clarity on what you are making progress toward and the benefits that come along with it. Move forward and don't let anyone or anything derail you from the amazing person you are creating.

Procrastination – Why do today what can wait until tomorrow? That is the complete opposite way of going about things. You have most likely experienced how a one-day delay turns into a week and then a month until you have that "oh crap" moment when what you were tasked with is now due. Change your mindset and take care of things as they come to you. With goals and creating your best life, what are you waiting for? There is nothing that says it has to be a certain date or month or new year or anything. When you make the decision that you want something different and are going to do things differently, start right then at that moment. There is no permission you need from anyone to get going.

Lack of Accountability – You set out items or goals or steps to complete along the way and when you don't reach them, you have no one there to call you on it or make sure you are doing what you said. The best combat here is if it is a friend, family member, or spouse, someone who may be taking their own path or a cheerleader, have them there to help with ensuring you are doing what you said. Also, make sure you have clarity on what you want and why, and stay focused. This will help prevent you from abandoning your progress.

Negative Self-talk – This goes right back to your mindset and how you view things. "I can't," or "I shouldn't," or "Why am I doing this?" should not enter your mind. Remember, this process is simple but not easy, it will be worth it as you continue to make and see improvements. Your mindset should be about positivity, learning, making adjustments, and focusing on what you are becoming and why, not on why it won't work. That is the old version of you, not the new version.

Lack of Time – This is the most common item that tends to derail people from changing the trajectory of their life. Responsibilities or other people's tasks for you will get in the way of your plans and actions. If it is a health goal to become more active, know that there will be times when you won't be able to get a walk or workout when you initially planned. That's okay. Have your game plan for when things like this happen. Have a different time to work out planned, or if you can't get out, make time to do an in-house workout. There is always something you can do to keep the needle moving forward. For most people, they miss a day, then the next week it's two days, followed by more time spent missing days than getting a workout done. And before they know it, they are no longer getting anything done and are already pointing to the next year. That isn't you. You have a clear vision and know why you are putting in this work, and your mindset of constant growth means you have alternative plans to make progress each day. None of those plans entertain the thought of missing a planned day.

Not a Priority – If living your best life and making progress is not a priority, the likelihood that you will make it happen shrinks to basically zero. Once you decide that you want something different and commit to doing things differently, make it a priority in your life and daily routine. Your future version of yourself will thank you for doing this. Don't dip a toe in the pool and think that you'll see how it goes. Instead, just jump in and tell yourself you are doing this, and when challenges present themselves, you'll figure out a way to keep going. We are all born for greatness, but few people ever attain it. The main reason is that people don't prioritize that daily pursuit.

Perfectionism – It is such a rare occurrence when things go exactly as initially planned. There are always adjustments and alternatives that need to be taken. When you put together your steps of how you will get from where you are to where you want to be, be detailed, but know that everything you have put down is not going to happen exactly the way you thought or planned for. This is where approaching every step with a thought of success or learning comes into play. When something doesn't go exactly the way you planned, it's not only okay, it's great. It gives you the opportunity to learn what didn't work and why, how you need to adjust, make that adjustment, and keep moving forward.

Previous Failures – If you have set a goal and didn't succeed in the past, the majority of people won't even entertain setting the same goal again. Don't let that be you. Your approach is different. You learned why it didn't work previously, and your attitude and mindset are in a better position this time. All of us have different experiences, things we accomplished and things we didn't in our past. Don't look back at those times and think of them as failures or allow them to debilitate your pursuit of your best life. They are experiences to learn from and keep you from making the same mistakes.

So far, we've covered challenges that are internal. These are the things you create in your own mind or that stem from your history. Some might have you looking outward for support, but most of them come from within. You might not face all of these, and there may be others unique to you, but whatever shows up, don't let it derail your journey toward becoming the new version of yourself. Learn from your past, but don't let it dictate your future.

Now let's talk about the external challenges, the ones that don't come from you directly, but from your environment, your situation, or the people around you.

Lack of Understanding – This one will come from friends, family, or people close to you who just don't get why you want something different or more than you already have. That's fine. Most people won't understand. What matters is that you do. It's not your job to convince anyone why you want something different. Like we said before, people will fall into one of three categories: cheerleaders who join you, cheerleaders who support but don't join, and those who don't understand and want to keep you where you are, because that's where they're comfortable. You get to choose who you bring with you on this journey. Just don't let someone else's confusion about your goals become a reason to stop. Your fire is lit. The only way to feed it is to keep making progress.

Peer Pressure – This comes from the people who want things to stay the same, not because it's best for you, but because it's comfortable for them. Your goal isn't to keep others comfortable. Your goal is to live your best life. People will come and go, and some of them won't want to see you grow. That's a reflection of where they are, not where you're going. Be honest about who belongs in your life and who doesn't.

Sabotage – This one's tough, because it often comes from the people who claim to care. You start walking after work, and suddenly they're scheduling things at the same time. You start eating healthier, and now they're inviting you out for burgers or drinks. Pay attention to their intent. Are they supporting your growth, or trying to hold you in place? Stand firm. If someone schedules something during your workout, say no, you already have plans. If they pressure you to eat or drink something you don't want, tell them no. You'll quickly learn who supports your goals and who doesn't. From there, the choice is yours, keep them in your life, or not.

Competing Priorities – This can be both internal and external. Internally, don't take on everything at once. You're building something for life, not just this year. Pick the goal that matters most and start there. Externally, you'll face demands from work, family, friends. Don't be a "yes" person. It's okay to say no. And if something truly can't be avoided, that's fine, you already have a plan to adjust. That's the beauty of preparing for challenges ahead of time. It doesn't throw you off. You're simply taking another path you have already planned out.

Dependency – Let's say your goal is to create a stronger, more loving relationship with your family. That obviously requires participation from them. Sit down with them before you begin and talk about your vision. But more importantly, ask questions and listen. Find out what's important to them, individually and as a unit. When everyone has a voice, they have a reason to stay committed. Now your goal isn't just your goal, it's your family's goal. And that's powerful. Any time your goal involves others, bring them in from the start. Show them you value their input. You're not just building your future; you're building it together.

Lack of Encouragement – Like with dependency, this one's about the people close to you. If they don't understand what you're trying to achieve, they may dismiss it or look at you like you're crazy. The key here is communication. Take a step back and think about who this involves and why it matters. Then talk to them. No need to tell everyone every detail, these are your goals, but the ones closest to you should know what you're working toward, why it matters, and where their encouragement might be needed.

Comparison – Let's face it, today's world is run by the internet, social media, and technology. Everything is right there at your fingertips. And with that comes constant images of success: the travel, the money, the cars, the homes, and all the amazing things people are doing. But here's the truth: that is not your comparison. The only comparison that matters is you versus the version of you from yesterday. Your goal is to grow by 1% every single day. That's it. That's your focus. Also remember, what you're seeing online is the highlight reel. People don't post the long nights, the stress, the effort, or the setbacks. Think of social media like an iceberg, you're seeing the top 10%, the polished part above the water. You're not seeing the 90% below the surface, where they're kicking, screaming and working their rear end off to keep that 10% afloat. No matter what your goal is or where you're at on the journey, remember, your only comparison is the you from yesterday. If you have wins to share, absolutely post them. I'll be cheering you on. But don't stop there. Keep kicking and screaming to keep that success above the waterline.

Conflict – Don't kid yourself, no matter how well you've thought things through or how clear your aspirations are, there will be conflict. Things won't always go as planned, and not everyone will see or agree with what you want for your life. That's fine and should be expected. Conflict doesn't always show up in obvious ways, it might be subtle or disguised as support. Not everyone or everything will support you as you level up and shift the trajectory of your life. Take it in stride. This is your life, your goals, and your vision. You know what's important and why. If conflict comes up, don't let it derail you. Learn from it and make adjustments if needed, but don't change course just because someone else is uncomfortable. Some conflict may come from jealousy or resistance to change. Listen, take what's useful, and stay on your path. Your goal is not to make everyone happy. Your goal is to fulfill the greatness you, and everyone else, were born with.

No Collaboration – Unless your goal is to build a closer, more loving and supportive immediate family, collaboration isn't needed. If your goal is health-related, that's for you and why it matters to you. If your goal is related to your job or wealth, those are also yours to own, and you control your actions. Sure, a promotion or raise depends on your employer, but that part isn't in your control, your effort and performance are. If it's wealth you're after, ask yourself: can I create it where I am, do I need to branch out, or take on a side gig that pays me? Only you can answer that. But as you craft your goals, be clear about what it's going to take, so the effort you put in actually moves you toward the results you want.

As I said earlier, this is a list of common challenges you might face, but it won't cover everything. The key is knowing upfront that challenges will come, and having a plan to course correct when they do. The biggest reason people give up is because they weren't prepared, they didn't expect obstacles and didn't plan for how to handle them. That's not going to be you. You want something different than you have now, and the only way to get it is to commit to doing things differently.

Do Different Now, ask yourself:

What challenges will you face?

Who are your cheerleaders that join you, cheerleaders who support you, or anchors that don't want anything to change?

Plan for each category?

Chapter 15

Alone

Prove Them All Wrong

We've talked a lot about challenges and the role other people may play, but in the end, these are your goals. This is your future. This is your decision to change for the better. It's not because someone told you that you need to, or because you hit a certain age or a stage in life that says now is the time to think about your future. None of that. It's a choice you make when you decide you're tired of living an ordinary life. You want more. You want something different than what you currently have. And most importantly, you recognize that the way you've gone after your goals in the past hasn't worked.

Don't be discouraged. Ninety-nine percent of people never figure out how to achieve their best life. Most don't even realize there's more out there than what they experience in their daily, never-ending cycle. You're already ahead of most just by recognizing you want more and understanding that doing things the same way you always have isn't going to suddenly work this time. A big part of real, lasting change is admitting there's more out there, realizing your old way hasn't worked, and accepting that if you want different, you've got to do different. Now that you've made that decision, the real work begins.

This is where doing it alone comes into play. People won't understand. They'll talk about you. They'll try to keep you where you are. Some may even get mean or nasty with their comments, talking behind your back or to others about what you're doing and why. Don't waste your energy responding. This is your plan. You've put in the work. You know what you want and why you want it, and nothing is going to stop you.

Let them talk. Let them say whatever they want. You don't need to defend yourself. Let your results speak for you. Stay quiet and keep making progress. You'll feel the shift. The noise might still be there at first, but fewer and fewer people will be listening. And eventually, no one will be listening. Why? Because they'll see your progress. They'll see who you're becoming.

The silence will be deafening. You haven't heard it in a long time because the comments, the doubt and the negativity were the fuel that lit your fire. But now your fire burns without needing anyone else's opinion.

Don't be afraid of going through this alone. The comments, the questions, the judgment, they'll all fade away. Because soon, your results will make it clear: you made the right decision when you chose to do things differently and go after the life you were meant to live.

Do Different Now, ask yourself:

Be clear that these are *your* goals and your future, how will you insure that they are *yours* alone?

Chapter 16

Success Stories

In addition to Katie, who I spoke about earlier, there are hundreds of success stories, people making progress, changing their lives in positive ways, and starting to live their best life. I won't share all of them, but a couple really stand out.

The first is Matt. He was in his mid-fifties when we met, just after the Covid pandemic had started to ease up and people could finally begin getting out again. We were talking about how we spent our time during lockdown. I told him that just a few days after everything shut down, I was still out walking and staying active, for my kids. Before this turns into some debate about safety, I'll just say I brought a mask, and the guideline was to stay at least six feet apart. The paths I walked were eight feet wide, so I kept to the rules.

Matt told me the pandemic had the opposite effect on him. He stayed inside and gained what he called "a great amount of weight." As we kept talking, he said he needed to get back in shape. I asked him why it was important, and who it was important to. At first, his answers were surface level. But then he opened up.

He told me about his two sons, how they used to play baseball growing up, and how he coached them. Those memories meant the world to him. Then came the spark, his fire. His sons are now married, and one of them was expecting a baby boy, the first grandchild in the family. Matt lit up when he talked about creating those same memories with his grandson. But he also realized that in his current state, not only wouldn't he be able to coach, he might not even be around long enough to try.

That thought hit hard. It became his reason. His fire. So he started walking and working with a trainer a couple of days a week. Even when it got tough, Matt didn't stop. He kept showing up. And now? He's not only in shape, but more active than ever. He's brought other family members along for the ride and is already planning to coach his grandson's baseball team when the time comes. Matt's success came because he found his real reason, and once he did, there was no stopping him.

Then there's John. His story is very different, but just as powerful.

He opened up quickly when we met. He was married, owned a successful construction business, and life was good, until it wasn't. His wife had been unfaithful. She took him to court, ended up with his company, and they divorced. Just when it seemed like things couldn't get worse, they did. The man she was with assaulted John, leaving him with broken bones and some brain damage. This had happened years before we met, but he was still struggling, especially with work and relationships. His goal, at that point, was simple: a return to normalcy.

We talked through what was most important to him, and he said employment, without a doubt. So, we looked at what hadn't worked and came up with a new plan. Instead of sending out the same old resume, John did something different. He asked a potential employer to meet him at a home under construction. He walked through the site, explained what he saw, how it was done, and how he could help. That one move landed him the job. He was promoted quickly after. His new approach helped him stand out, and it worked.

I've stayed in touch with John over the years. Today, he has more responsibilities, he's spoken with the company owner about having some ownership, and he's thriving in a new relationship with someone who fills his heart and supports his journey. They cheer each other on, every step of the way. When I met him, his life had been knocked down hard. But he found clarity.

He took a different path. And because of that, everything changed.

These are just a couple of stories, but there are so many more. People can, and do, change their lives for the better when they get clear about what they desire and find the right way to go after it.

Do Different Now, ask yourself:

What does your success story look like?

Chapter 17

Conclusion

In the end, when you get to the point where something sparks you to want a different life, or it builds up over time from doing the same thing over and over, living the same day on repeat, and you finally make the decision to set a goal and change the trajectory of your life for the better, there is a process. It's simple, but not easy.

First comes your mindset. This will take some deep self-work and honest evaluation of what has worked in your past and what hasn't. It starts with your outlook, how you feel about your future. Do you tend to focus on the positives in each situation, or the negatives? Do you believe that your effort can actually make a difference, or do you feel that outcomes are already decided for you?

When challenges hit, and they will, will you adjust and keep going, or will they cause you to quit again? How do you feel about doing something new? Are you willing to try, or do you let fear shut it down before you even begin? Do you dwell on your past? If things haven't gone your way before, are you letting that stop you from trying again?

How do you see yourself and the life you're capable of creating? Do you believe that, with the right plan, attitude, and support, you can actually live your best life? Or do you think your story is already written?

Most importantly: do you see success and failure as the only two options? Or do you understand that it's either success or learning? Because no one truly fails. You just get the chance to learn something new. Some of those lessons are small, some are massive, but they're all part of the process.

When you shift your mindset to view everything as a learning opportunity, you're more likely to keep going instead of giving up and waiting for next month or next year, or when you feel things are perfectly aligned. Here is the thing, they never will. The perfect time is when the thought first enters your mind. Take advantage of this opportunity inviting you to succeed.

Once your mindset is right, once you're focused on what *will* work instead of what won't, now you're ready to map out your goals and go to work. Start by thinking about what your best life actually looks like, health-wise, wealth-wise, and relationship-wise. Those are the three main areas people set goals around. And most people, including you, will likely have more than one.

Begin with the one that's the most pressing in your mind, the one you've struggled with the most, or the one you're most ready to face. Start there. You'll feel a deeper sense of accomplishment and positivity as you make progress.

Keep in mind: you are designing your *lifetime*, not for the short-term. A common trap is setting goals that solve for the short term without considering what life will look like years from now. Also, don't cut your goals short, don't think small. Think big, then go even bigger. If the goal feels too big, good. It will require multiple steps, but we'll get to that shortly. Setting goals that seem too high or too big puts you in the mindset of figuring out different ways and things you can do to keep making progress toward that ultimate goal. Think about what it will feel like as you make progress and as that goal gets closer and within reach, it will inspire you, keep you going, and have you looking for more. In the end, the goal you initially set for yourself, which may have seemed too big, will now feel too small, because you were meant for more. Once you get your goal in place and your mind is right, the next step is to figure out the why. Why is this goal important? Why does it matter to you? Who else does it matter to?

Ask why at least five times, like your grade school English teacher taught you, to get to the real answer. This is what transforms motivation, which is fleeting, into inspiration, which is a fire that burns deep inside of you. That inspiration becomes your fuel.

For me, I started with a weight loss goal and became more about being able to play and be active with my kids. If they came home on a Friday and said they wanted to go camping over the weekend, I didn't want to be the father who handed them gear and told them to have fun, I wanted to be the father who loaded up the truck and said, "Let's go."

As I walked each day, I never even looked at the scale. I didn't care. It wasn't about the number. It was about how I felt, what I was doing, and who I was becoming. Losing weight became secondary to being active, and something I could and continue to do every single day and for the rest of my life.

This is an important step, asking yourself and uncovering your true why. Why is this goal important? Who is it important to? Is it something you can see yourself doing consistently for the rest of your life? It doesn't matter what the goal is, there's a reason you desire it. That reason is what lights the fire and drives your progress. And most of the time, your real why doesn't have a lot to do with the goal itself. If your goal is a certain amount of wealth, odds are it's not really about the number, it's about the comfort, the memories you want to create, or maybe even the fact that growing up, you didn't have it. You've got to dig in and find *that* reason. Ignite that fire inside and go after that reason no matter what gets in your way.

Once you've figured out which goal tops your list and why it's important to you, it's time to design your path and figure out how you'll get from where you are to where you want to be. Here's a tip I like to use: don't start your steps at the top of the page, start at the bottom. Your life is building up, not down. It's just a small trick to play on your mind as a reminder.

There's not a step too small or insignificant. Depending on your goal and where you're starting from, this could include a lot of steps. Don't let that dissuade you. Each step is forward progress. And here's something most people forget, celebrate every success. Whether it's reaching a level, hitting a milestone, or just doing what you said you were going to do that day, celebrate it. That momentum will keep you moving.

Write down as many steps as you think you'll need to take. Remember, this is your goal for a lifetime, not a short-term fix. If you have a thousand dollars now and your goal is to become a billionaire, it's going to take more than a couple steps to get there. Be detailed. Be realistic about what's needed and how long it might take. Understand that no matter how solid your plan is, you'll have to make adjustments. You will face challenges. Some you've seen before, others will be brand new. But with your mindset positive and learning built into your process, you're already prepared to adjust and keep moving forward.

As you are designing your path to your huge goal, look back into your history and ask: why haven't you done this before? What derailed you in prior attempts, and why did you give up the moment it got a little tough? If this is something new to you, what challenges could you face and how will you adjust? Don't look at this as a way to avoid obstacles and challenges, they will always be there. They'll show up at times, in situations, and from sources you hadn't even considered. Do your best to think of all possibilities, but also expect the unexpected. Learn from them, adjust, and keep pushing forward. The purpose of identifying some of the "why nots" is to have a plan for when they do come up, but also to realize that you can't think of everything, no one can. The mindset you put yourself in, of looking for the positives and being open to learning, will help you not only handle the unknown, but be happy it showed up. It's an opportunity to learn something new and come up with creative ways to keep making progress.

Lastly, think about the future and when you get to a point of achieving, or almost achieving, your goal, what's next? Your mind, body, and spirit will thirst for it and want the next goal to go after. As we said before, this is living your best life in all aspects, and there is more than one thing you most likely need to get there. Go back to when you first started thinking about it, what was the next most important or most challenging item you thought of? Start the process over. In all likelihood, you may have already started that path while working on your first goal.

I'm sure you've heard the saying, "a rising tide raises all ships." The same is true here. As you made progress and started achieving a better version of yourself in the specific goal you were tackling, other items on your list most likely moved higher, and you saw improvements there too. Think of it like this, if your initial goal had something to do with wealth, your relationships most likely improved as well. Not because of the money, but because of the person you were becoming. You became an attractor. People sought you out because of the positivity you had and the purpose that now drove your life and actions.

The beauty of going about it this way is that when you reach success and are ready to start the next aspect of your best life, your mindset work is already done. You know how to craft your goals and find your why. Now it's about laying out the steps to get where you want to go. The obstacles and challenges will still be there, and new ones will come, but you've learned how to handle them and are better equipped to adjust and keep moving forward.

To get started and make progress toward living your best life is straightforward, and we've covered as much as possible in this book. First, start with your mindset. Stay positive and know that every experience is an opportunity to learn. Set a goal, not a small one, but a big one, something worthy of your lifetime. Then figure out your why. What's the real reason you want this? Who is it important to, and why does it matter that you achieve it?

Next, lay out your path. What steps do you need to take to move from where you are now to where you want to be? Look back and identify what has stopped you in the past. What obstacles might come up again, and how will you adjust when they do? And finally, ask yourself: what's next? What's the next item on your list that matters for your best life? What progress have you already made, and what still needs to be done?

At its core, this book focuses on two things. First, simplicity. We tend to overcomplicate things, piling on extra steps and losing ourselves in the process. The approach I coach cuts through the complications and eliminates anything that may be wasting your time. It's simple. It doesn't require a ton of time, energy, or overthinking. Just commit to getting 1% better every single day. That's it.

The second thing is this, if you want different, do different. If you want something new or better in your life, don't fall into the trap of repeating what hasn't worked. That will only lead you back to the same results, and another year stuck in the same place. We were all born for greatness. You deserve to live yours. But it's not going to happen by doing the same thing over and over again, hoping for something to change.

So don't wait for the calendar to tell you when to begin. Don't wait for a season or some big external event to give you permission to start. Your best life is waiting for you to claim it. If you want different, do different.

Now, GO!

Do Different Now, ask yourself:

What are your takeaways and plan?

Resources

Scan QR code for the Mindset Quiz, the Pre-Program Homework and the Program Worksheet

Downloadable Resources

About Todd Baker

Todd grew up like most kids in Colorado, playing football and baseball during the school year, baseball all summer, and skiing all winter. After high school, he went on to play junior college and college baseball, but when his senior season ended, so did his baseball career.

He started off in his field, business, but quickly realized that sitting in a windowless office typing all day wasn't a great fit. He pivoted to bartending for the money and soon after stumbled into the mortgage industry, thanks to one simple phrase he saw in an ad: "limitless income potential." That moment launched his journey into self-employment.

Over the years, Todd's career spanned mortgages, new home sales, and real estate. But through it all, one thing stayed constant, his obsession with learning and self-development. He devoured everything he could get his hands on: personal growth, leadership, motivation, mindset, you name it.

Eventually, that path led him into personal development coaching. He knew he wasn't the only one trying to figure out how to level up in life. His mission became clear: help people and businesses gain clarity through simplicity. A lot of the lessons he's learned, through experience and growth, have been poured into this book. His hope is that it opens eyes and reminds people of one powerful truth: the biggest limitation we face is ourselves.

https://calendly.com/project9life/30?month=2025-06

- facebook.com/todd.baker.54922169
- instagram.com/project9life
- linkedin.com/in/transformationcoachtoddbaker

www.ingramcontent.com/pod-product-compliance
Lightning Source LLC
Chambersburg PA
CBHW062114080426
42734CB00012B/2854